Disney
FROZEN
TOP 10s

SOME PEOPLE ARE WORTH MELTING FOR

MARY LINDEEN

LERNER PUBLICATIONS ◆ MINNEAPOLIS

For Laura and Carol, my
beautiful sisters —ML

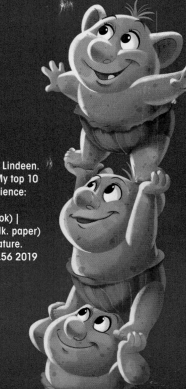

Lerner Publications Company
A division of Lerner Publishing Group, Inc.
241 First Avenue North
Minneapolis, MN 55401 USA

For reading levels and more information, look up this title at
www.lernerbooks.com.

Main body text set in ITC Avant Garde Gothic 13/14.
Typeface provided by International Typeface Corp.

Library of Congress Cataloging-in-Publication Data

Names: Lindeen, Mary, author.
Title: Frozen top 10s : some people are worth melting for / Mary Lindeen.
Description: Minneapolis : Lerner Publications, 2019. | Series: My top 10
   Disney | Includes bibliographical references and index. | Audience:
   Age 6–10. | Audience: K to Grade 3.
Identifiers: LCCN 2018013057 (print) | LCCN 2018014090 (ebook) |
   ISBN 9781541543614 (eb pdf) | ISBN 9781541539112 (lb : alk. paper)
Subjects: LCSH: Frozen (Motion picture : 2013)—Juvenile literature.
Classification: LCC PN1997.2.F76 (ebook) | LCC PN1997.2.F76 L56 2019
   (print) | DDC 791.43/72—dc23

LC record available at https://lccn.loc.gov/2018013057

Manufactured in the United States of America
1-45094-35921-7/17/2018

TABLE OF CONTENTS

SOME THINGS ARE WORTH THINKING ABOUT

OLAF SAYS HE'S "ALWAYS LOVED THE IDEA OF SUMMER AND SUN AND ALL THINGS HOT." He really likes everything about the season. Or, at least, he really likes the *idea* of it. Olaf has never actually experienced summer, so his opinion of it might change. And that's OK. Opinions can change. Opinions are what you think or feel about things. One day you might really be in the mood to build a snowman. The next day you might want to go ice-skating. Your opinion about how you want to play in the snow can change.

But facts don't change. Facts are things that you can prove to be true. For example, when Olaf says he doesn't have a skull . . . or bones . . . that's a fact. You'll find lots of facts and opinions in this book. See if you can tell which is which.

**JUST TURN THE PAGE
AND GET STARTED!**

FROZEN'S TOP 10 FROZEN THINGS

10 The village water fountain.

9 The forest on North Mountain.
IT'S THE PERFECT PLACE TO BUILD AN ICE PALACE!

8 The waters of the fjord.

7 Marshmallow.

6 The stairway leading to Elsa's ice palace.

5 Snowgies!

OUR FAVORITE PART OF *FROZEN FEVER*!

4 Anna.

BUT DON'T WORRY. SHE DOESN'T STAY FROZEN FOR LONG!

3 All of Arendelle until Elsa learns to control her powers.

2 Elsa's ice palace.

1

OLAF.

THAT IS, AS LONG AS HE STAYS AWAY FROM FIRE.

TOP 10 REASONS ANNA IS A GOOD SISTER

10 She likes a lot of the same things as her sister. **LIKE CHOCOLATE AND PLAYING IN THE SNOW.**

9 She's musical. **SHE'LL EVEN SING THROUGH A KEYHOLE IF SHE HAS TO SO SHE CAN TALK WITH HER SISTER!**

8 Anna never blames Elsa when her sister has a hard time controlling her powers.

7 She's caring.

6

Anna doesn't let other people's fear change how she feels about Elsa.

DID YOU KNOW?

The filmmakers who worked on *Frozen* interviewed women about what it was like to grow up with a sister. They wanted to make Anna and Elsa's relationship as accurate as possible.

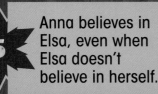

5

Anna believes in Elsa, even when Elsa doesn't believe in herself.

4

Anna is determined to help her sister no matter what other people say.

3 She's brave.

ANNA IS WILLING TO FACE DANGER TO RESCUE HER SISTER.

2

Anna loves to play, especially with Elsa.

DO YOU WANNA BUILD A SNOWMAN?

1

ANNA LOVES HER BIG SISTER.

TOP 10 TIMES ELSA WAS STRONG

10 When she takes off her gloves at the coronation ceremony.

EVEN THOUGH SHE WAS AFRAID HER POWERS MIGHT BE REVEALED.

9 When she gives Anna advice about Hans that Anna might not want to hear.

8 When she accepts her responsibility to become queen after her parents pass away.

WHAT A BIG RESPONSIBILITY.

7 When she decides to live on a lonely mountain on her own to keep the people of Arendelle safe from her powers.

6 When she makes an entire ice palace by herself.

HER POWERS ARE SO AMAZING!

∧∧∧∧∧

DID YOU KNOW?

Frozen's animators designed a special snowflake for Elsa that appears throughout the movie. It's on the doors to the balcony of her ice palace.

5 When she fights off Hans and the Duke's men when they come to the ice palace.

4 When she uses her icy powers to let the citizens of Arendelle play in the snow and ice.

MAKING AN ENTIRE ICE RINK IS NO SMALL THING!

3 When she breaks through the wall of her prison cell.

2 When she learns to live without her parents even though it's hard.

1 WHEN SHE FINDS THE COURAGE TO STOP HIDING WHO SHE REALLY IS.

11

FROZEN'S TOP 10 MUSICAL MOMENTS

10 A chanting chorus rings out as Arendelle finally thaws out.

9 The ice harvesters deliver a cold warning about a frozen heart.

BRRRRR!

8 Kristoff and Sven's "duet" about reindeer versus people.

7 The trolls "fix up" Kristoff.

THEY ARE SOOO HELPFUL!

6

Anna begs Elsa to come back to the kingdom, and Elsa begs Anna to just leave her alone.

5 Olaf imagines what summer would be like.

JUST THINKING ABOUT IT MAKES HIM SO HAPPY!

4 Anna and Hans open the door to love and maybe even marriage.

WAIT, WHAT?

3 Anna is so excited on coronation day that she can hardly stand it!

2 Anna sings into the keyhole to ask Elsa to come out and play.

1 ELSA DECIDES TO LET GO OF HER FEAR AND BE HERSELF.

TOP 10 OLAF QUOTES

10 "Oh, look at that. I've been impaled."

9 "Hands down, this is the best day of my life . . . and quite possibly the last."

HE SAYS AS HE'S MELTING.

8 "Love is putting someone else's needs before yours."

7 "Why isn't she knocking? Do you think she knows how to knock?"

IT'S WHAT'S BEHIND THE DOOR THAT'S MAKING HER NERVOUS, OLAF.

6 "I like warm hugs."

5 "I always wanted a nose! It's so cute. It's like a little baby unicorn!"

OR A SNACK FOR SVEN—BE CAREFUL, OLAF!

4 "Whoa, so this is heat. I love it. Oh, but don't touch it!"

3 "And who's the funky-looking donkey over there? . . . And who's the reindeer?"

ANNA AND OLAF MAY HAVE HAD A SLIGHT MISUNDERSTANDING THERE.

2 "Oh, I don't know why, but I've always loved the idea of summer and sun and all things hot."

1

"SOME PEOPLE ARE WORTH MELTING FOR— JUST MAYBE NOT RIGHT THIS SECOND."

FROZEN'S TOP 10 DRAMATIC MOMENTS

10 — Elsa's quick change into her new icy dress.

9 — The Duke's men shoot at Elsa in the ice palace as she fights them off.

8 — Grand Pabbie warns young Elsa about her powers.

7 — Kristoff and Sven race back to Arendelle to save Anna.

HURRY, KRISTOFF!

6 Young Elsa accidentally hits young Anna in the head with ice.

THE FIRST SIGN OF TROUBLE . . .

5 Hans reveals his plans to kill Elsa. Then he locks Anna in the cold library.

NOT A GOOD GUY AFTER ALL!

4 Elsa accidentally freezes all of Arendelle.

3 Wolves chase Kristoff, Anna, and Sven through the forest.

2 Marshmallow chases Kristoff, Anna, and Olaf off a cliff.

1

ANNA SAVES ELSA'S LIFE BY BLOCKING HANS'S SWORD JUST AS SHE FREEZES.

DOESN'T GET MUCH MORE DRAMATIC THAN THAT!

QUIZ BREAK!

How many fabulous *Frozen* facts do you know?
Take this quiz to find out!

1

EVERYONE KNOWS WHO OLAF IS. WHAT IS THE NAME OF THE OTHER SNOWMAN ELSA CREATES TO PROTECT HER ICE PALACE?

A Snowball
B Marshmallow
C Rocky
D Frostor

2

WHAT IS ANNA AND ELSA'S FAVORITE FOOD?

A Cupcakes
B Chocolate
C Carrot cake
D Cherry pie

3

WHICH FROZEN CHARACTER SAYS, "ICE IS MY LIFE"?

A Oaken
B Marshmallow
C Elsa
D Kristoff

4

WHO SAYS, "THAT'S NO BLIZZARD. THAT'S MY SISTER"?

A Anna
B Elsa
C Hans
D Kristoff

5

WHICH REAL-LIFE PLACE ON EARTH IS THE INSPIRATION FOR ARENDELLE?

A Norway
B Sweden
C Denmark
D The Netherlands

6

WHEN ANNA AND ELSA OPEN UP THE CASTLE FOR ELSA'S CORONATION, WHICH FAMOUS DISNEY PRINCESS IS AMONG THE GUESTS?

A Aurora
B Rapunzel
C Merida
D Belle

7

WHERE DOES ELSA CREATE HER ICE PALACE?

A North Mountain
B The South Pole
C Dark Valley
D The Far Peak

HOW DO ANNA, KRISTOFF, AND OLAF GET TO THE DOORS OF THE ICE PALACE?

A An ice slide
B A secret passage
C A long staircase
D By climbing a wall

8

9

WHO CONVINCES KRISTOFF TO GO BACK TO ARENDELLE TO HELP ANNA?

A Elsa
B Olaf
C Sven
D The Trolls

WHAT ACT OF TRUE LOVE SAVES ANNA FROM AN ICY FATE?

A Kristoff coming back to save her
B Olaf starting a fire
C A kiss from Hans
D Anna jumping in front of a sword to save her sister

10

FROZEN'S TOP 10 OUTFITS

10 Anna and Kristoff dressed in troll fashion, wearing capes and headdresses made from plants.

9 The Duke of Weselton's coronation outfit.

INCLUDING THE FRINGE AND WHITE GLOVES THAT HELP HIM SHOW OFF HIS DANCING SKILLS.

8 Sven's antler accessories from the frozen forest.

7 Oaken's Nordic knitwear.

6

Hans's coronation outfit.

IT MAKES HIM LOOK LIKE ONE OF THE GOOD GUYS, DOESN'T IT?

∧∧∧∧∧
DID YOU KNOW?

Animators studied the way real fabrics felt and moved as they designed the outfits for *Frozen*. Then they could make computer drawings of clothing for *Frozen* that look and move just as real clothing does.

5

Kristoff's no-nonsense mountain man clothes.

4

Anna's warm winter travel clothes.

SHE KNOWS HOW TO BUNDLE UP IN STYLE!

3

Anna's coronation gown in shades of yellow and green.

THE WARM, FRESH COLORS OF SUMMER.

1

2

Elsa's coronation gown, in darker, cooler shades of winter.

ELSA'S ICY GOWN, CAPE, AND SHOES.

IT'S THE ULTIMATE COOL OUTFIT!

TOP 10 THINGS TO DO IN ARENDELLE

10 Learn to harvest ice.

9 Enjoy a ride on Kristoff's fancy new sled. **BRING A CARROT FOR SVEN, AND ENJOY THAT CUP HOLDER!**

8 Hike to the realm of the trolls. **WATCH OUT FOR THE ROCKS!**

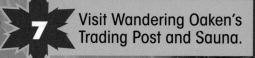

7 Visit Wandering Oaken's Trading Post and Sauna.

6

Meet lots of interesting people down by the water when ships come in to port.

5 See the northern lights.

4 Go to a ball hosted by Anna and Elsa.

3 Take a tour of Elsa's ice palace.

CAREFUL ON THE STAIRS—THEY'RE A LITTLE SLIPPERY.

2 Say hello to a friendly snowman who travels with his own personal flurry.

1

GO ICE-SKATING ALL YEAR.

DON'T FORGET TO PACK YOUR SKATES!

23

OUR TOP 10 FAVORITE THINGS ABOUT *FROZEN'S* TROLLS

10 They are good singers.

9 They wear cloaks made of moss.

8 They can grow mushrooms on their bodies.

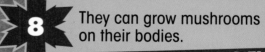
HOW DO THEY DO THAT?

7 They are small, but they can roll and stack themselves if they need to be taller.

6 Their crystal necklaces glow. **THEY LOOK JUST LIKE THE NORTHERN LIGHTS!**

^ ^ ^ ^ ^
DID YOU KNOW?
The swirling designs on the trolls' clothes are meant to look like lichen. Lichen is a small, slow-growing plant that lives on rocks and trees.

5 Family is very important to them.

4 They can make themselves look like rocks. **ROCK ON, TROLLS!**

3 They can organize a wedding in a hurry.

2 They are love experts. **DO YOU NEED A HEALING HUG?**

1

THEY ARE KIND AND WILL HELP ANYONE IN NEED.

TOP 10 REASONS WHY KRISTOFF IS AWESOME

10

He knows how to harvest ice.

ICE IS HIS LIFE!

9

He's always prepared for winter.

8

He's an excellent sled driver.

7

He eats healthy food.

A LOT OF CARROTS . . .

6

Anna and Elsa realize that true love can take many forms.

∧∧∧∧∧
DID YOU KNOW?

Walt Disney wanted to make a movie like this for a long time. He first thought about it in 1943, but *Frozen* didn't come out until 2013. Sometimes it takes a long time to get a story just right!

5 Elsa realizes she can be herself without being afraid.

4 Kristoff and Sven rush through the storm and across the frozen fjord to save Anna.

3 Anna uses the last of her energy to save Elsa.

NOW THAT'S TRUE LOVE.

2 Elsa comes to understand that love is stronger than fear.

AN ACT OF TRUE LOVE IS STRONG ENOUGH TO THAW A FROZEN HEART.

1

OLAF WARMS ANNA BY THE FIRE (AND HIMSELF JUST A LITTLE TOO MUCH) AS HE EXPLAINS TRUE LOVE.

MAKE YOUR OWN *FROZEN* TOP 10!

WOULD YOU LIKE TO MAKE A *FROZEN* TOP 10 LIST?
Ask an adult to help you make a copy of the blank list on the next page. Then make your own *Frozen* Top 10. You can rewrite one of the lists from this book. Or you can make a whole new list instead, such as the

TOP 10 REASONS OLAF WOULD BE A GREAT BEST FRIEND

Or think of the

TOP 10 PEOPLE IN YOUR LIFE WORTH MELTING FOR

That would make a great list! Use your imagination to come up with more cool ideas!

MY

Disney

FROZEN
TOP 10:

10. Goldie is my
9. Bestie ♡
8.
7.
6.
5.
4.
3.
2.
1.

TO LEARN MORE

Books
Dichter, Paul. *The Night Sky: A* Frozen *Discovery Book.* Minneapolis: Lerner Publications, 2019.
Explore the night sky with Anna, Elsa, and their friends. Learn about the northern lights, the stars, and more.

Pirotta, Saviour. *The Snow Queen.* Minneapolis: Quarto, 2017.
Read all about a young girl's search for her friend, who was taken by the Snow Queen. The story of Anna and Elsa is inspired by this fairy tale by Hans Christian Andersen.

Websites
Disney *Frozen*: Official Site
http://frozen.disney.com
From crafts to videos to games, you'll find Olaf, Anna, Elsa, and all things *Frozen* at this website.

The Story of *Frozen*: Making a Disney Animated Classic
http://abcnews.go.com/Entertainment/fullpage/story-frozen-making
-disney-animated-classic-movie-25150046
Find out more about how *Frozen* was made, and meet some of the people who made the film in these behind-the-scenes video clips.